Kids Are Weird

And other observations
from a pediatrician

Erin McArthur, MD

PUBLICATION CONSULTANTS

We Believe In The Power Of Authors

PO Box 221971 Anchorage, Alaska 99522-1974
books@publicationconsultants.com — www.publicationconsultants.com

ISBN: 978-1-63747-110-4
eISBN: 978-1-63747-111-1

Library of Congress Catalog Card Number: 2022918815

Manufactured in the United States of America.

Dedication

To my favorite weirdos
Sadie and Adam

Contents

Chapter One

From The Beginning

Birth to 2 months

I have had the honor and privilege of meeting thousands of souls within the first 24 hours of their arrival to this earthly existence. Twenty minutes was the soonest I saw any babies other than my own, and I felt the moment's magic. We all do two things from the time we show up here: pout and stretch. These visceral and involuntary reactions to the world around us are there from the beginning. Eyes wide open and bright, looking around at all they had been hearing over time. Right from birth, a mom can feed her baby to soothe them, at the breast or with a bottle. A dad has his voice. The voice they have been listening to from inside. Dad's voice is very different in tone, quality, and cadence than mom's voice. Mom smells

7

like milk from the breast, formula spilled on them while making bottles, or spit-up in their hair. Mom means food. It can feel frustrating as it seems you are given the baby every time you turn around and are told they are hungry. However, it is lovely to have a solution, no matter how temporary it may be! Luckily dads have their voice.

After the first feeding and dad lecture, babies are on their way to knowing their people and for their people to know them. It does not take long for new parents to figure out what their baby's "normal" looks like. This knowledge applies to things like normal temperature when touching their baby, normal eating habits, normal cries and what they may signal, and which diaper filling sounds will mean they need a bath. Trust in the parental gut is also there from the beginning, and you will find me referring to it often. If something feels different or off, you should ask someone or reach out for guidance and help from your medical professional. You may not even know why you are not liking what you are seeing or feeling, but if it feels off, it deserves your attention and effort to put your mind at ease.

My favorite question from well visits while I was in practice was for parents to describe their kid's temperament. It sometimes told me more about the parents than the kids, but overall, I loved hearing how parents describe their children. We all show up with our temperament. From those first 24 hours, it is apparent what kids are like. If they come out screaming at you, they tend to keep screaming at you. When they are calm and mild, it usually sticks as well. Nothing to worry about if you have a screamer. Knowledge is power, and you can use this to your advantage when you work with them through their life and all the obstacles and opportunities it holds! As medicine gets more into algo rhythms for solutions, children remind us we are all individuals, going through this life at our speed and with our strengths and weaknesses. The key is harnessing strengths and working with and despite weaknesses. Even though I will be giving some generalizations through this exploration of my observations, individuality is a theme running strong in the background. Build on the junction of your kid's ideal and reality!

The first day is a whirlwind. Often there is little sleep for anyone, dad included. People come in the room at all hours, asking about feedings and diapers and taking vital signs. It is exhausting. Before the time of covid, there was also making sure family members had a chance to visit and not feel slighted and get some rest for the new parents. The lack of hospital visitors has been good for families to bond with their latest edition, even if it is number 5 and especially if it is number 5. It may be the only alone time mom and dad get with the little one for years! Do not be afraid to ask for privacy if hospital visitor restrictions ever liberalize. Nurses I have worked with are great at telling family members it is time to leave. They take the burden from you, and they do it well!

The first 24 hours are hit or miss with feeding. This will surprise you with how often you are asked how the baby is feeding. It is important to offer milk to the baby every 2-3 hours, but if they are not interested, you can say you tried. Being born is rough for everyone involved, and sometimes babies need rest! And so do mom and dad. If the baby is sleepy in the first 24 hours, then enjoy it. It is not going to last! After the initial 24 hours, feeding every 2-3 hours becomes more critical, and you should step up your efforts a bit to feed the baby.

The second 24 hours are home to the most challenging part of this journey. Once you make it through the second night, you have made it through the worst part. Fourteen years later, I remember this second night so vividly. I was crying, my son was crying, and his dad was snoring. During night number two I thought, "how am I ever going to do this?". I am not going to lie; those thoughts continue to appear to this day in my mind's musical, thriller, comedy, and drama circus. Sometimes, a feeding finishes, and the baby is milk drunk. Mom is smiling like it is the most beautiful and natural thing in the world. Then the next feeding, everybody is crying, like ugly crying--what a rollercoaster. Hold on through the crying and enjoy the smooth rides when they appear.

And so begins life with a newborn. Eat, sleep and poop. These are all you care about now. You will even take a picture of a dirty diaper; it is your future! The next few weeks are all about feeding. The most important lesson is waking your sleeping baby is okay. Whether they need it or not, a diaper change is an excellent way to get a baby awake to feed. Most babies will wake themselves to eat, but I never want it to go unsaid; it is okay to wake a sleeping baby when it has been a while since they fed. More often, what you find yourself saying is, "you cannot be hungry. I just fed you!" You will utter this phrase a few times a day for the first 2-3 weeks, which is normal! Babies often cluster feed and feed for half an hour and are hungry an hour later. They do this a few hours in a row, and sometimes you get a little sleep after the feeding frenzy. If a baby sleeps 4-5 hours once in a 24-hour period, enjoy it. The first thing you say when you wake up should be, "boy, that felt good" then the panic of if everything is okay can get in until you see your sweet baby sleeping like a baby. Then you can get them up to eat and relieve the pressure in the breasts! At about three weeks of age, you will see how someone can breastfeed and still have any kind of life or even take a shower. The cluster feeds stop, and you feel there is more of a routine and schedule even to feedings. It must get better. People do it again! At about two weeks, there is a growth spurt, and when you think you cannot breastfeed any more in a day, they want more. There is another growth spurt at age six weeks. After a few weeks of a more scheduled and sustainable breastfeeding pattern starting around three weeks, a baby is suddenly eating like a newborn again. All . The. Time!!! This burst of feeding frequency is how they get mom to make more milk; through more emptying for a few days!

Milk generally comes in between the 2nd and 5th day. Many moms are worried about not giving their new babies enough volume of milk. The first few days are colostrum which has a different composition of fat and proteins than breast milk and serves a different purpose. It is thick and sticky, and I think of it as lining the intestines, frozen in utero, and tickling them awake instead of flooding them awake. If we were meant to have milk from the moment a baby was born, we would. Not having a lot of volume of milk from the beginning is by design, and some babies patiently wait for milk, while others do not. Another example of temperament being there from birth. Of course, milk coming in takes longer if you worry about it, but for most people, it is coming, and you cannot stop it. Minimal to no breast changes in pregnancy and fertility issues are potential signs of eventual low milk production, but there is no guarantee. Tiny boobs can make a ton of milk, and big boobs can have very little. It also takes longer for milk to come in when moms have higher blood pressure or swelling. I usually tell moms their milk will be in when their shoes fit again. Make sure to follow the baby's weight with your medical provider in those first few days after you leave the hospital.

After milk is in, there should be a half an ounce to one ounce of weight gain a day. Adequate weight gain tells us there is milk there, and the baby is getting it! If weight is an issue or latch is an issue, seek guidance from a lactation consultant. A bad latch is evident by persistent pain after a baby latches. The initial pain hurts pretty bad but should only last a few seconds. If you are gritting your teeth throughout the whole feeding, saying, "I can do this. I can do this." it is a bad latch. Get the baby off and try again. You may need to try a few times to get them on properly, which is okay. It is worth it. I think this is possibly the singular example of when our instinct as mothers is not quite right as moms want to suffer through it if it is a bad latch. It tears up nipples, making it hard to keep going, and the baby is not moving much milk with a bad latch. It is doing neither one of you any good. If the baby, and you, are getting anxious and antsy, go skin-to-skin on your chest and let everybody get a reset. Then try again. Even though skin-to-skin will reset parent and baby, there is a difference in how young and old express their anxiety in this feeding situation. Babies will open their mouths and shake their heads back and forth right at the nipple. I mean right there at the nipple, lips grazing the spicket to the liquid gold which is mom's milk! A mom will start to feel her shoulders go up, her neck muscles tighten, her jaw may tighten, and tears well up in her eyes. Skin-to-skin works every time.

Except when it does not. You cannot get relief from engorgement by skin-to-skin alone. There are times when everyone is asleep at the time milk comes in, and breasts get full and rock hard. It is the difference between trying to latch onto a watermelon versus a water balloon. If there is not some give to the breast, good suction cannot be achieved. Not all women feel the fullness and heaviness of engorgement. For those who do feel engorgement, not all will get to a super hard watermelon stage. Sometimes you need to fully empty the breast with a pump session and start over again. Sometimes you can soften the front part of the breast by pumping a little but not completely to empty. You can also hand express some of the front milk to soften the breast around the nipple and areola which is the prime latch location! Hand expression is very counterintuitive. Pulling out like you are milking a cow never works. We feel like cows, but alas, we are not. Pick the breast up and think about pushing it to the back of the rib cage. Squeeze down on the areola, the dark part around the nipple. This motion compresses all the milk ducts and is how you can squirt milk across the room if you want to. Heat before feeding or pumping and breast massage during emptying can also help alleviate engorgement.

Breastfeeding is certainly a topic you can get a lot of advice about. Most of the stories you hear from the public are very specific to the individual's breastfeeding experience. These experiences may be very good or very bad. So-so breastfeeding experiences are small in the fraction split of the whole. When you turn to a lactation consultant, you should welcome many different suggestions and recommendations. Parents are often frustrated with the variety of options for help. However, all of these different ideas are proof there is no one way to do anything! Lactation consultants are very busy, meaning you are not alone if you need their help. We do not always have access to our lactation consultants of the past (aunties, grandmas, mothers, sisters). Luckily there is a profession of people who can help when there are problems. There is a lot of emotion tied up with breastfeeding. When there are difficulties of any kind, it can make a mom feel like a failure, which is unequivocally not true! Use your village; the sooner you, as a mom, learn help is good, the better off you will be. "Doing it all" is overrated!

If you are bottle-feeding, it does not seem there is as much cluster feeding, but there may be some. A more significant question with bottle feeding is how much to give? There is no one answer to this for every baby. There is talk about how big the baby's stomach is, but I have seen some babies pack it away and seemingly want more! The first few days are usually 15-30 ml at a feeding. After every 15 ml you can stop and try to burp and see if they still want more. Do this every 15 ml. Over the first few weeks, you get a good idea of the amount they always take. Once they start to want more after a feed which in the past would satisfy them, you can take it up another 15 ml or so for the next feeding and top off as they want it. If they get more than they need, they spit it up, and, generally, no harm is done other than laundry. If spitting up or feedings seem painful for the baby with arching and fussing, see your medical provider.

These ideas are how I approach bottle feeding with formula or breast milk. As a shout-out to moms using bottles for breast milk, I believe pumping to feed a baby this way is a feat of great persistence and effort on a mother's part! I think it is the most challenging way to feed a baby. It will work best if you can simulate the baby's growth spurts by pumping a couple more times a day for a couple of days when the baby is eating more. More emptying means more milk!

A note about burping; new babies are not great burpers! This is especially true in the first week. You can try burping but do not feel like you must go on until you hear the sweetest little belch sound you will ever hear! If a baby is comfortable, there is nothing more you must do other than get them upright for a bit and see what comes of some taps on the back. If they are bothered by gas bubbles, you can try to bicycle their legs as they lay on their back. You can support their chin and back of the head while they "sit" on your knee and gently stir them in circles to help move the gas bubble. If gas pains are all day long, associated with painful feedings, or interfere with feeding, see your medical provider.

In these first few days, there is also a frequent phenomenon called brick dust. There can be an orange pinkish discharge or spot in the diaper. It is not bright red like fresh blood. A parent once described it to me as terracotta, and I thought it was a brilliant way to picture its color and texture. These are urate crystals and they show up in urine when we are a bit dehydrated, waiting for milk to come in. These crystals are not a sign of damage to the kidney, and dehydration is part of a normal process of the first few days while the gut gets primed for more food. If there is poor feeding along with the presence of crystals or any concern about the baby's weight gain, follow up closely with your medical provider.

Although it feels like eating is all your newborn is doing, sleep is a big part of a newborn's life. Some people have called the first few weeks after birth the 4th trimester.

There is still a lot of brain growth happening during sleep. The variation between what babies need for sleep is much larger than when kids are older, like when they are teenagers. There is no one answer to how much sleep a baby should get. It is a lot, though. Remember, they only do three things, and eating and pooping are relatively quick endeavors. Recently I heard about an idea of a wake window which made a lot of sense to me. As we get older, we get into trouble when there is a missed opportunity to go to bed, and we get our "second wind." These second wind times are not peaceful and smooth because our awareness was not supposed to be awake. The length of time to get into a second wind seems pretty quick for babies, maybe even as little as 60 minutes of this wake window. The key is to smile and nod when everyone tells you about the schedule they got the kid on as a baby. It had everything to do with the baby and not the parent.

Focus your attention on your knowledge of your baby. You know best what they, as an individual, need and what their cues are. Most babies do not have a circadian rhythm time frame to the day until age 6-8 weeks old. No matter what we do as parents, our kids decide to be asleep at night and awake in the day in their own time, but most will be there by eight weeks of life. Living in Alaska can be hard when it is always light in the summer. My suggestion to families has always been to be quiet and to dim the lights in the evening and night. Then do the daytime activities in the day and with the lights on, even if the baby is sleeping. Babies will get there when they get there!

I never get too excited about sleep habits for the first few months. Starting at four months, I begin talking about self-soothing to sleep happening by six months of age. Babies are babies for such a short time; enjoy holding and snuggling while they nap in your arms as you stare at your child's wonder.

After the sweet thought of holding your baby while they sleep, imagine the blowouts where you feel the warmth growing on your palm while cradling their cute little bum. The last of the newborn trio of life events is poop. As you will see over the years, the answer is always the poop to almost any problem or life's question. Even if you never could talk or think about poop in the past, this will change after you have a baby. My husband, the one home with our kids when they were younger, said he would need a mask, goggles, and gloves to change diapers. I knew he would have to get over the disgust real fast! Sometimes in the newborn period, you change 10-12 diapers a day, a lot of them with stool! Baby poop is all diarrhea. It is like this until they start solid foods. Stools are liquid to pasty. Some stools seem like they are all water, which is fine. I care less about the frequency of stooling in the newborn period than I do about the consistency of the stool. A nugget stool is constipation in a newborn, and my first thought is they do not like dairy (either in the formula or in the mom's diet). You can try a sensitive formula or a hypoallergenic formula if formula-fed. Dairy (milk, cheese, yogurt, ice cream) out of mom's diet requires an elimination, but I think of it as more of an exchange. With the elimination of dairy, a mom loses fat, protein, calcium, and Vitamin D from her diet. Practicing in Alaska for so long made me realize the importance of extra Vitamin D for all Alaskans, drinking milk or not. This need could also be the case for the lower 48. Still, a mom should talk with her medical provider to see if they need more Vitamin D. Vit D molecule does not easily get into breast milk. A mother's intake of Vit D in foods is often not enough for an exclusively breastfed infant (in Alaska, we even give extra Vit D to formula-fed infants). You can find protein in leafy greens, meats, beans, fish, and eggs. Calcium is in leafy greens and almond butter/almonds, and fat is in avocados, olive oil, nut butters, and coconut milk. The coconut milk in the can has the most fat and is a wonderful addition to smoothies. This type of coconut milk is what makes Thai ice tea taste so good! If the baby is doing better after some time (every couple of months, maybe), try adding a small amount of dairy back in and see if the baby tolerates a threshold of dairy. Cheese a couple of times a week may be fine, but every day may be too much! Find the threshold of exposure the baby tolerates in hopes of preventing anaphylaxis reaction with future exposures.

I have seen a rainbow of colors of baby stools, and before the days of cell phones, people brought the diapers into the office. Surprising even myself, I always wanted to see it! I care most about three stool colors: red, black, and white. Red is new blood, black is old blood, and white is a lack of bile. Green stool by itself is less concerning to me if there is good weight gain and no gas pain/painful stooling for the baby.

Not all babies change the frequency of their stooling, but if it happens, it is usually around one month, and a baby may go a whole day or 2 or 3 without stooling. They are not constipated if they are comfortable, eating well, and the next stool is soft. So much information on a baby's well-being goes back to feeding, weight gain, and comfort. If there is pain or poor weight gain, be sure to be working with your medical provider to figure out what is going on and how best to help.

Random tidbits. Mom can have Ibuprofen again. Yay!! There is an excellent resource most pediatricians will have regarding mother's milk and medications. Check with your pediatric provider about any medications mom is taking while breastfeeding. I have seen moms following instructions to pump and dump when taking a medication, not out of any science but due to the adult provider not knowing if it is safe. Always good to ask an expert! As far as over-the-counter medications, a breastfeeding mom should be cautious with the use of decongestants and antihistamines. Their purpose is to dry up, and they can also dry up milk supply. These medications are dangerous to supply.

Hiccups and sneezes are normal and do not mean anything. If a baby hiccups a lot in the womb, they tend to keep doing it when they get out. Feeding sometimes brings it on and sometimes makes it better. Overall, it bothers us more than it bothers them. Sneezing is how they keep their nose clear so they can eat and breathe simultaneously. (side note- no matter how mashed their nose looks in the breast, if they are eating, they can breathe. Breathing wins every time! No need to mess with their lips, the latch, or your breasts if there is no pain for mom and the baby is happily eating).

Girls will have a mucousy vaginal discharge, and you can leave it alone. You can spread things apart to get out stool, but the slimy stuff can stay.

Lotion will not help the dry skin. The babies just got out of a nine-plus month-long bath. They must peel the top layer of skin; they basically have to molt. Suppose the creases get red and irritated looking, usually at the ankles. If this redness happens you can apply Vaseline, coconut oil, nipple cream, Aquaphor, or shea butter as examples. I only say to use these products if the skin looks more irritated. Another baby skin issue in the first couple of months is baby acne. This acne looks just like…wait for it…..acne! Cute little pinpoint pimples. They can be red dots or even yellowish pinpoint dots with a slightly red base. They come and go with good days and bad days. Taking pictures on the good days is the only advice I have on the matter. There is nothing to do about it. It generally starts around 2 weeks, is at its worst between 4 and 6 weeks, and is gone by 8 weeks. The presence and severity of acne as an infant is not a crystal ball into their teenage skin's future.

Every day with a newborn brings new experiences, questions, and confusion. Babies change so much in the first year and have so many strange normal things happen! Blocked tear ducts present themselves in this neonatal period. Like acne, there are good days and bad days. The bad days have a watery, crusty, or yellow/white stringy discharge. The tears are welling up since they are not draining, and they crystalize. The difficulty in tears clearing the debris, their real job, can be a setup for an infection. If the drainage gets thick and green or there is redness in the white part of the eye, this may need medicine to treat a bacterial infection. You should also seek medical care if poor feeding accompanies the drainage. Of course, under two months, a fever (anything over 100.4 degrees Fahrenheit) needs immediate medical evaluation, meaning a trip to the emergency room if this temperature elevation occurs in the middle of the night.

You will never be faulted for feeding your baby. Feeding your baby is the number 1 job and protecting your milk supply if breastfeeding/using breast milk is the number 2 job. I see laziness over nipple confusion, so if everyone is crying at 2 AM and your instinct is to give the baby a bottle, then give them a bottle! If laziness develops you can fix it over time. Always feed the baby! Make sure to empty the breast if you are not putting the baby on the breast; emptying a breast is how you protect the milk supply. It is a demand-driven supply. Like a pail of water, you cannot put more liquid in until you empty the previous liquid!

If you are a breastfeeding mom, please eat and drink! A dad's breastfeeding job is to keep mom fed and watered!

Breastfeeding efficiently without harming the mom takes 500 extra calories a day. For some moms, I cannot even find 1000 calories in what they have eaten all day. Often, moms drink enough water as they are very thirsty, but a whole day can go by, and the baby (and any other children) have eaten so well, but mom has not eaten a thing! Part of it is you are not hungry and the other part of it is there is no time! You do not need to have large meals. Get bang for your buck when you are eating. Toast with butter and peanut butter, a handful of nuts over a handful of crackers. Smoothies with coconut milk and extra olive oil on veggies. Think fat and protein!

The last part of the newborn period is to remember there is a mom and dad (or a mom and mom or a dad and dad) who are still people. This period is the strangest transition time with no owner's manual and minimal sleep. Not the best setup for success but luckily, the first few weeks do not need a lot of variety. It is just that you are doing something at all times. It is a time for cruise control and subconscious direction. My keyword for the first two weeks, especially, is survival. Everything you thought you would do as a parent goes out the window, and you just try to get through the day, sometimes through the hour. When you are up at 2 AM pleading with your 2 week-old to sleep in a bassinet, know many other parents of 2-week-olds are standing over a bassinet too. They also have their hair a mess, their clothes with spit-up, pee and poop on them, begging and crying for their sweet creation to take a lesson from Samuel L Jackson and go the @$&% to sleep!

The haze will end, you will remember parts of it, and some of your memories will even be true! You will amaze yourself with what you can do with so little sleep and wonder how you ever spent your time before this little person showed up. All you do now is stare at them, their wonder, their perfectness. You will be sure those little smiles are just for you until you get your first purposeful smile. It's a game-changer when the true interaction starts. You were hooked before, but now you are smitten. You can do this!

CHAPTER TWO

Interaction and Personality

2 months to 6 months

"She is finally fun!" And no, this statement does not sound bad. It is a very truthful statement. From birth to the 6-8 week mark, there has been a lot of work and not a ton of interaction from the baby. You have spent most of your waking hours over the last few weeks doing for, thinking about, or looking at (a combo of all three in reality) this precious life in front of you. As lovely as it has been, it has been work. Now you get smiles and purposeful interaction. You talk, they talk. You smile, they smile. They have arrived and are taking in the outside world more than just the basic needs of eat, sleep, and poop. They are tracking you as you walk by, reacting to your face and voice more connected and meaningfully. One of the dangers of being a pediatrician mom happened when my son was three weeks old, it was shocking to me how little a newborn does. I was convinced my son was just a brain stem, the area of the brain that meets these basic needs. Of course, I saw in time the higher parts of his brain were indeed present. They have been developing as he interacts more with this world and environment. And he really arrived in this world about eight weeks of age.

Along with this interaction, you get the beginning of movement. By age 2 months, babies have the movement of the face mastered with smiling. These next couple of months is a time to work on the chest strength to help get to the next step of rolling over. Tummy time, as long as everyone can take it, will help develop this chest strength. Rolling over usually happens between 3-5 months. Infants are no longer safe left on the couch or a bed! You never know when the first roll is going to come. We get a lot of calls when the first roll comes right off the couch. Usually, the baby is fine, but the mom is a mess! When you must step away, put the baby on the floor. If there are older siblings or pets, on the floor right in front of you while taking a bathroom break is the most preferable!

Drool often becomes a big part of life from 2-4 months. Are they teething? Yes, they are always teething! The drool and chewing happen for a long time before teeth pop through. The first tooth can show up anywhere from 4 months to 18 months, a vast normal range. Somedays, there is even a little bubble on the gums, and you think, "here it comes!". The next day it is gone! You know the tooth has arrived when the little razor blade bites you. My biggest takeaway with teeth is anything goes. They will seem to skip teeth as far as the order of arrival but know the ones in between will show up eventually for almost everybody. You can have a kid at one year of age with no teeth and a kid with a whole mouthful of teeth, and they are both normal. I have told many people I would get x-rays if there were no teeth by 18 months just to prove they were there. I never did this in 20 years of practice. Teeth always appeared by then. If kids are happy drooling and chewing, they do not need pain relief for teething. Try different things as well. I have seen kids get relief from a cool, wet washcloth or the handle end of a silverware spoon. I would not think a spoon handle would be soothing but to each their own. Avoid numbing agents to treat pain. Theoretically, they can numb the airway if the medicine gets down lower. Too much can make it difficult for oxygen to get around in the body.

This early infant age range is usually home to a feeling like you have a routine and a little bit of a handle on how to do this whole keep a kid alive thing. 2 to 6 months can bring peace, tranquility, and confidence. It can also open the flood gates to the relentlessness of raising children. This relentlessness is especially true at an age they are entirely dependent on you for every aspect of their life. A basic idea of being overwhelmed by this endeavor is if you cry more than the baby. This amount of crying is not a good sign. Other red flags for a mom are a decrease or increase in appetite, an increase in fatigue, and poor sleep. These last two symptoms can be challenging to evaluate in the postpartum period. It is concerning if the symptoms are worsening. If all aspects of your life are in trouble (family, work, and friends), there is a deeper problem than you may realize. Ideally, we catch when we need help before it gets to this point. Often moms feel they will be fine if they make it to 2 months without feeling depressed. However, the 4-month time is a particularly common time for parents to have issues with depression. Seek professional help if you are worried about depressive feelings or symptoms.

Dads can be affected in this postpartum period as well. I have seen this most often in times when a dad does not feel comfortable with the daily cares of an infant. Changing some diapers can bring a dad and a baby so much closer, enhancing bonding. The dad (or non-primary caregiver/provider) and the infant are better for the connection.

During this period, there are not many changes in the caretaking of an infant. Continue to feed on demand, there is still lots of poop, and you will see more smiles and rolling over. Tons of personality traits come out, but they are not very mobile. These attributes make this my favorite age! They get good at helicopter scoot and just rolling in general, so you must be quick if you sneak into the kitchen. Still, overall, they stay pretty much where you leave them. The life of a four-month-old is to have their hands in their mouth, drooling, and doing crunches. Their job at this age is to develop core strength. They are trying to be sitting up without being so tippy closer to 6 months of age, and they need to build those abs!

The concept of eat, sleep, and poop can probably be a way to look at all stages of life. At age 2 to 6 months, life is for sure still this simple. Eating consists of breast-feeding or bottle-feeding formula or breast milk. You are still feeding on demand, although it is not uncommon to have a routine to timing and amount of milk at a feed. It seems waiting until six months of age to start solids puts them at the best set up to have a sound gut barrier in place. This waiting will likely help with food tolerance. This school of thought may change just as we used to wait to give peanut products until age 3 (if allergists had their way), and now we say to give it early and often, one of the first foods.

Stay tuned to your health care professional as we continue to learn over time. The current recommendation is to wait until as close to 6 months for food. Regarding the idea of being an individual, there is nothing magic about age 6 months that will make every kid ready to eat (from a gut standpoint, interest standpoint, or a mechanical ability standpoint). There is watching you eat and diving after your food while you eat. These actions are signals of interest level. You can try things off a spoon once they start diving after your food. If they just tongue thrust it back out, they are not mechanically ready to eat (to get their tongue around the food bolus and move it back in their mouth), and you should wait a week and try again. Regarding gut readiness, I think waiting four days or so between each new food can help you determine if they tolerate a food. If there is a lot of gas pain or stomach pains, or rash with the food, then you can take it away and re-challenge again in the future. With many new foods at once, you would have to take them away and give them back one at a time for any problems anyway, so you might as well do it slowly from the beginning. They need medical attention if there are true hives or welts after eating a particular food, swelling, or difficulty breathing. No extra water until after 6 months of age, even if they are taking some foods before this time.

Sleep at this age is still relatively blissful. Get babies to sleep and enjoy the times they sleep a little longer. Breast-fed babies are usually still getting up at night to feed. Consistently sleeping 6-8 hours at this age could affect milk supply. Remember that emptying the breast is what gives room to make more milk. With less frequent emptying overnight, the supply gradually weans down to accommodate the decrease in demand. If weight gain is going well, you can keep supply up with pumping between the last feeding and the time mom goes to bed. If weight gain is not going great, work with your medical provider to look at how to make sure sufficient weight gain occurs.

There is no age at which all babies will be sleeping through the night. If this were the case, there would be no need for the dozens and dozens of sleep books out there. As with breastfeeding advice, this is another case where there is more than one way to do things. It is not that one sleep book has it right. Some sleep books will speak to you more than others. One common truth is sleep changes between 6 months to 3 years of age, and it becomes normal to wake and stir in the middle of the night. The goal is not to involve you! To prepare for this common sleeping change, you can try to develop self-soothing for a baby by 6 months. This strategy means a baby goes down relatively awake and puts themselves to sleep. Whatever you do to get a baby to go to sleep will be what they need to go back to sleep when they wake (which you can expect after 6 months). If you hold their pinky until they go to sleep, when they wake up, they hold up their pinky for you to hold on to and get them back to sleep. If music is playing or a light mobile is on, it must go all night. The baby needs to wake up and say, "yep, everything looks and sounds the same as when I went to sleep. I will put myself back to sleep". This concept is your best bet to get your baby to sleep through the night (of course, they did not sleep through the night, but this ignorance is bliss!).

Between 4 to 6 months, I suggest putting the baby down at bedtime slightly awake, and see what happens. If it does not work, you can pick them up, feed them or rock them to knock them out and try the next night again. They may surprise you! Do this every night to reach the goal of self-soothing by 6 months of age. They likely will need something when they wake up until 6 months of age, but you will have set a sound stage for a time in the future when they wake and may not need anything. Now, if your infant/toddler has developed self-soothing after 6 months and continues to wake at night and need you, this is just the sleeper they are. The good news is it will change like a light switch when it changes. One night they will just sleep through the night. The problem is it will never be soon enough. It may be between 2 and 3 years of age even. Survive the middle of the night and continue encouraging self-soothing at bedtime.

Special situations are when the infant/toddler is in the same room as the parents and especially when they are co-sleeping. These variables are often too strong to overcome with any traditional conditioning parenting technique. If you are breastfeeding, they wake up and smell mom, it is hard for them not to want a quick bite to eat, hungry or not. Also, if they are co-sleeping, it is not too safe when they are younger to have them in the bed without you for them to fall asleep initially. Ideal and reality, find the intersection and make it work!

And finally, poop. This part of life is still about the same as it has been since one month of age until they start wanting more solid/pureed foods. Food is a poop game changer! I have heard people say that baby stool smells yeasty, especially breast milk stool. Either way, it is generally not offensive. However, once food enters the picture, our olfactory senses will be keenly aware of a change. There is also a tendency for the stool's consistency to change. If pellets develop, I think more of true constipation. At this point, a child's stooling has everything to do with what they are eating (probably true for adults as well, but my medical knowledge certainly takes a hit at age 22!). The usual constipating foods at this age are bananas and rice or rice cereal. The P fruits will soften things up easily. Peaches, pears, plums, and prunes. And yes, infants and toddlers will, for the most part, eat prunes. Juice can work for this, but real food is a better option than a compressed version full of calories. Also, after 6 months, be sure to offer water after eating solid foods. Offering a couple of ounces of water in a sippy cup once they get the concept of a sippy cup or out of a bottle until this time comes will help keep their stools softer. Their kidneys know what to do after 6 months of age, so if they get more water than they need, they will just pee it out.

Random tidbits. A word about growth charts. At the well visits, your medical provider will show you growth charts for weight, length, and head circumference. One of the keys to these charts is the range from the top line to the bottom line ideally encompasses 95% of kids in the US. It is best to pick a line and stick to it. Some kids are at the bottom of the chart, and some are at the top. The key is to stay on a line as you follow a healthy lifestyle. There is a different chart from birth to 3 years than used from 3 to 20 years. It is impossible to extrapolate much from the birth to 3 year chart into adult predictions of height or weight.

Although all the ages are fun, this one is all-around great. The parents feel they are getting the hang of a few things, there is a little more sleep for everyone, and the kid has not said "no" yet! So much personality, not very mobile. However, regarding mobility, do not be lulled into too much complacence. The couch and bed are not safe places to leave the baby!

This period is also the age of the Michelin tire baby for some; lots and lots of rolls! When your 4-month-old gets stinky, look in the folds. The neck and armpits are the main culprits for holding drool, milk, and sweat. If there is a little pinkness, you can apply thick and white diaper cream to help keep the moisture out and prevent yeast. If the area keeps getting more pink/red you can use an over-the-counter antifungal cream twice a day for a week or so. These creams are in the foot section of the store and are generally used to treat athlete's foot.

The biggest takeaway from this age is to develop self-soothing to go to sleep by the 6-month mark. Everybody will sleep better!

Chapter Three

Feeding and Chasing
6 months to 12 months

Six months of age, you made it a half a year. It is a feat, and kudos to you. You have survived the most sleepless of nights (until daycare colds seep in), and you get so much interaction and play with your little one. And they are still not terribly mobile, most of them at least. As you move into the second half of the first year, it is time to focus on feeding and chasing. And, of course, there is always more poop! Once again, the first year of life is more forms of eat, sleep, and poop. But now we must think about mobility as well. A new challenge for sure!

The most common time to start feeding an infant solid food is 6 months. The basic thought process behind this is the gut barrier is strong and can handle the deluge of food proteins entering the intestines and not react poorly to them. As I stated, some kids are interested in and have been eating more solid foods (not breast milk or formula) before 6 months of age. Most infants, though, will show their interest and be ready with regards to mechanical movement of the tongue closer to the 6-month mark.

I always wished there was a chart for what food to give, what amount, and how often. Sadly, there is no such resource. Every kid is different, and every meal for the same kid is different! Initially, feeding is practice. One new food every few days is the consensus to help identify foods they may not tolerate. Some intolerances do not show up for a few days, but you can figure if they handle a particular food after four days, they will continue to tolerate it. Initially, solid foods are once a day or as often as they demand you feed them when everyone is sitting down to eat. At 9 months of age, you are consistently feeding three meals a day and a couple of snacks. I have no idea how you get from feeding one meal daily to three meals and a snack. In reality, every day is different. One day is more about milk and the next day is more about solid foods. Following their lead is the only real rule.

There is a movement of feeding called baby-led weaning. At its most basic, this entails kids in charge of their feeding, eating foods they can handle on their own, and skipping the pureed stages of foods. I have seen successful feeders from baby-led weaning and parents feeding infants off a spoon. I have seen kids develop a good relationship with foods both ways. Use the method which speaks to you. The key for all of it is to follow the kids' lead. When their bird mouth is open, you keep feeding them or letting them feed themselves. They are done even when they only have 2 bites, close their mouth, and turn their head. No honey is the only absolute no for food before a year of age. There are botulinum spores in honey that an infant's gut under the age of 1 will take up, and the infant will get botulism. Allergists have changed their tune for food introduction in the most recent past. They are recommending fewer restrictions for potentially allergy-producing foods. Other than no honey, size and texture is now your only limiting factor. Creamy peanut butter is good, but peanuts are a choking hazard. Eggs, strawberries, and the typical allergy-producing foods are now being thought of in the feed early and often category to prevent future reactions.

Adding food directly to an infant's gut changes the game regarding stool. Smell changes, as you can imagine, and the consistency also does. It is essential to keep track of stool consistency at this age and make diet changes to keep stools soft. Kids are smart, and if it starts hurting to pass a stool, they will begin to hold it in. This withholding action takes months to develop, but it can take years to fix! Best to not even go there! I find rice, rice cereal, and bananas to be the most constipating foods creating harder stools. Feeding any P fruits (peaches, pears, plums, and prunes) can mitigate this. Some kids do well with a daily prune to help keep things soft. Water becomes another factor in keeping stools soft. After the age of 6 months, an infant's kidneys can dilute and concentrate urine. They can tolerate ingesting water without it diluting the salts in their body. Offering a couple of ounces of water after eating solid foods can help keep stools soft. As mobility increases and they master using a sippy cup, the infant can make their way to the water in a cup on the coffee table. Thirst drives this action.

A quick note about sippy cups: they seem like such a user-friendly invention. They are not! This age is when every parent innocently tilts up a sippy cup with the thought of showing your prodigy how easy fluid can get from a cup to your stomach. You will start contorting your face and sucking like there is a fast-food chain milkshake on the other end of the straw! Try different cups is all to be said here. It feels like there are as many cup styles as stars in the sky but keep trying them. Either one will work, or your kid will eventually be old enough to use a regular cup. You can always tip a regular cup to their mouth from time to time to get water in while they practice. I also encourage the use of water in the sippy cup. First, none of us need juice. A pear will help soften stools just like pear juice but without the concentrated calories. Secondly, when the inevitable spills happen, you can pleasantly say, "I am so glad we drink water in this house." The non-sticky factor alone sells water even if the whole "source of all life" thing does not do it for you!

I realize I changed the order here, and we have talked about eat and poop but nothing about sleep yet. As you add solid foods, the impact on stooling is so dramatic it had to skip the line. Pay attention to the stool just as you do the nutrition; they go hand in hand. Of course, everything is easier to handle when you have some sleep! It's not uncommon that you have been reacquainted, at least a little, with sleep at this stage. Even a breastfed infant may only be waking once a night (or even not at all) by now. However, everything changes at 6 months of age. Infants have a regular sleep change where they begin to wake and stir in the middle of the night. This change is a natural occurrence from 6 months until 3 years of age. The goal is not to involve you in the middle of the night when they wake/stir. To self-soothe back to sleep, they need to know how to self-soothe to sleep initially at bedtime. As discussed in the last chapter, the goal is self-soothing at bedtime by 6 months. They then will more seamlessly make this sleep transition without interfering with their (or your) sleep.

If the infant has not developed self-soothing by this point, there is still time. Focus all your attention on bedtime and survive the middle of the night. There are a lot of sleep books out there, and they are all right. You need to look at the one which speaks to you and your kid. I like the kinder, gentler cry-it-out method of checking on your infant with your hand on their back while making Shshing sounds. Then, after a bit, make the same sounds while standing at the crib's edge. After a bit longer still, make the same sounds again but now outside the door. There is no correct answer for how long to wait before going in to check on them; it is what feels right to you as a parent, knowing you and your child better than any book out there. The key becomes consistency. Find a method you can stick with for a bit. It is important to remember the 2nd night will be the worst, and they will pull out all the stops to get you to come in. You will want to say, "This is never going to work," but hang in there. You can do it. By the 4th or 5th night, most kids figure this is the new way of doing things. A more willful child may take a couple of weeks to adjust. The most willful child in my practice took a month to self-soothe. It was a hard month per mom but ultimately worth all the struggles. Remember that whatever you do to get them to sleep is what they will look for to go back to sleep. I will admit I do not have any good advice for co-sleeping families and sleeping, especially when breastfeeding. A midnight snack is effortlessly in front of their face. Would you turn down a bite of something you loved if you groggily awoke to find it in front of your mouth? Luckily there are enough sleep books to go around for all the sleep situations and strategies for everyone to find one which is acceptable.

Some tips about the crib. Sometimes I feel a little trapped in my bed with the aches and pains of the years settling into my bones. Infants and toddlers are trapped in their cribs, at least for a brief time. One of the schemes to get our attention is to take off their zipper sleepers. This new skill is adorable until they get it off with their dirty diaper, and you must clean the crib at 2 AM. Code for cribs has so many bars, so close together now. Of course, it has nothing on cleaning a car seat after a puke fest, but we will leave that for another discussion. If you have a onesie-footed sleeper Houdini in your house, and let's be honest, who doesn't, cut the feet off the onesie and turn it around with the zipper in the back. Go to bed with the diaper and clothes in the correct place. Wake up the same. What a concept!

More crib talk. Kids will pull to stand most often between 8-10 months. Anything they can look into; they can tumble into. 6 months is a great time to get the crib mattress lowered. As they bring themselves to standing and the crib railing hits them just below their belt line, they tend toward a headfirst dive over the crib railing. You can avoid this action with the mattress in a lower position, so the railing hits them at the upper chest. There are many babies with larger heads than others, but, all babies at this age have disproportionality large heads! You will also witness this exaggerated headfirst motion of the baby as they become more mobile.

6 to 12 months have glimpses into a mobile child's life. 6 months looks to have solid sitting up without being so tippy. Pulling to stand is usually 8-10 months and letting go and taking steps is 12-14 months of age, after the first birthday. Crawling often happens in this time frame but not always. Occupational therapists like people to crawl before they walk, but pediatricians do not care. I am not sure who is right, probably the occupational therapists. Still, mobility intensifies on either the knees or elbows or one knee and one foot or 2 feet. Your quick

trips to grab something in the other room needs to be faster, and your eyes need to multiply to see all the potential hazards before they do. Childproofing is a long game; it is a dynamic, fluid event. Sometimes it happens in real-time, sometimes in the morning after you awake in a cold sweat thinking about the strings on the blinds behind the couch. I have realized the bottom drawers in the kitchen are a favorite so having them empty or full of Tupperware is a good idea. Keep the bathroom door closed. Toilet locks keep all people out, and sometimes, you must use the bathroom quickly. The last thing you want to encounter is a toilet lock with a bladder in a body that has recently given birth!

A vital lesson to learn early is nothing is ever out of reach. In the 6-to-12-month period, there are many gross motor gains, including climbing. They can figure out what to move together and how to engineer their way to whatever shiny object has their interest in those 10 minutes. One family had the idea to zip tie a kitchen chair leg to the table leg to keep the infant from using the chairs as ladders. Infant's engineering plans become more sophisticated with their gross motor increases and better planning abilities.

As mobility increases, the best discipline at this age is to remove and distract. As the infants go towards the electrical outlet, you move them to their toys to play. They go back, and you move them to their toys; again. At some point, they do not want the outlet or object they are going to (dog bowls, cords, plants). They just want the game with you. Block them from the thing but do not interact or look at them. They will get bored and find something else to do to get your attention and eye contact. Play defense but do not look them in the eyes!!!

Eye contact is what they are often after at this age, and they are experimenting with different behaviors, trying to see if they get eye contact out of it or not. What you say and how you say it does not matter. They will often bite your shoulder or hit you while you are holding them on your hip. They smile and beam if you look right at them, even while you use a stern voice and say no. They got you to look at them. Say, "No, biting hurts," then put them down and turn your back on them. This reaction has the most meaningful impact in learning the behavior will not get them the desired result, eye contact. This strategy works when kids are biting other kids too. Say no to the biter and turn your back on them and shower the one bitten with attention. The caregiver's lack of eye contact and attention is the opposite of what the biter is after.

Along with gross motor development, you will see fine motor development. A pincer grasp, an ability to use the index finger and thumb to pick up things, shows up in this six-month time frame. It would be nice if they used this skill for picking up items and putting them away or into the trash. However, this skill usually gets dangerous small objects into your child's mouth to scare the daylights out of you and remind you that you can still sprint when needed. You will learn you are not afraid to stick your fingers in someone else's mouth. It does not matter when you last vacuumed or swept; your child will find the most miniature items in the most obscure places. Childproofing is one thing when you have one child. Childproofing becomes another beast when older siblings have barbie shoes, legos, beads, and slime. Of course, I am all for keeping the kids' toys in one room, door closed, and no baby entrance. Ideal yes, reality probably not so clean. Survive; you can do it!

Language development at this stage consists of more consonant sounds like gaga and baba. These sounds do not mean anything. An infant will go up to a chair and say ma-ma-ma, and they are just playing with their voice. After 9 months, you will realize they are starting to understand what you are saying even before they say the words themselves. At a year of age, look for mama and dada more specific and one other word.

Tidbits. At 9 months of age, many kids have started in a daycare setting, and colds have begun their coup in your household. I am always amazed how kids can get viruses even when the family "never goes anywhere." Even at the beginning of covid, when we were in quarantine and people were legitimately not going anywhere, kids were still getting viruses. They are tenacious little buggers; viruses and kids alike! Kids seem to get a new cold every three weeks because they do. They will often get worsening symptoms over the first 5-7 days and then improve over the next 5-7 days. They are well ever so briefly, then the next round begins. My bar is low; 2-3 days of wellness generally means a new virus when symptoms appear again.

When kids get common illnesses like colds, stomach bugs, and an ear or sinus infection here and there, I worry less about the immune system. In these cases, the immune system is working; it is just being asked to do a lot. I am more concerned if a kid has weird infections like an infected lymph node needing to be drained by a surgeon or four episodes of pneumonia in one winter. These occurrences should prompt you to have a discussion with your medical provider to consider looking closer at how well the immune system functions. Remember, the best help for the immune system is real food, healthy food, good sleep, and decreasing stress as much as you can. Like most things in parenting, this is much easier said than done. Still, if you try your best, you can revel in the good days and be happy at the end of any bad days once they are over and know tomorrow is full of potential.

I would frequently get asked if we separated well visits and sick visits. In theory, this sounds great, and some offices have excelled at this separation. The problem I always found is rarely is a kid, especially in late infant to toddler stages, well at their well visit. They often are just starting, just getting over, or in the thick of a cold. You may hear, "there is no ear infection, just a little fluid behind the ears." If you constantly hear this phrase at well visits, even with colds, make sure to bring this up with your medical provider. This is an age when prolonged fluid behind the ears can present just as many problems as recurrent infections. When ENT (Ear Nose and Throat) doctors put tympanostomy tubes in kids with prolonged, persistent fluid behind the eardrums, they call it glue-ear because the fluid is the consistency of rubber cement. Therefore, it has never drained; it is too thick. The structure of the head under age 3 inhibits adequate drainage of mucous from behind the eardrums, contributing to these problems. This period is critical for language development as they start saying more sounds and multiple sounds together. When kids hear things muffled like they would with a lot of thick fluid inhibiting the eardrum's movement, the risk is they will speak muffled. I often hear parents tell me they are not worried since they can tell their kid hears fine. The worry is they may not be hearing all the decibels. They may be missing key decibels which make them miss syllables or sounds when listening to spoken words. Although I often encountered chronic fluid behind the ears from 9 months to 2 years of age, it can happen at any time, and I have had teenagers get tubes in their ears for chronic fluid. Make sure to bring up to your care provider for any age kid when you feel you are always hearing they have fluid behind the ears, even if they are not having a lot of infections.

9 months of age is one of my favorite developmental milestones of object permanence. This is another level of interaction with their surroundings. When you hide an object behind your back, they will start to look for it. Before this age, the object would be out of sight and out of mind. Peek-A-Boo is a favorite game that emerges at this age as they have an idea of "hiding" things, but they still exist. This newfound interaction with the world

also shows up during their well visits. I have noticed at 6 months of age, an infant will often crunch the table paper. After all, it makes a delightful noise. At 9 months, there is another level of interaction with the world, and not only does it make noises when you scrunch it, but you can tear the paper. 6-month-olds are noisy with the paper, and 9-month-olds destroy the table paper.

CHAPTER FOUR

Where did you go and why are you so fast?

12 to 18 months

A whole year has gone by; where did the time go? The years go by fast (even though some days creep by, never-ending). It is time for smash cake and a birthday party which is more for the parents who survived the first year than the guest of honor. You now have a full-fledged toddler, and life will never be the same!

There are minimal food restrictions at this age. Size and texture are what limit food at this point. They can have all foods if they can handle them in their mouth. The first tooth comes in any time between 4 months to 18 months, so there is a vast range of normal, and there can be kids at a year of age with no teeth and kids at a year of age with a mouth full of teeth. They are all normal. The gums are hard, and you know this as they have bitten you. They can handle food even without teeth yet. You will know the tooth is through when the little razor blade gets you where there was once the dull hardness of only gums.

They can have all dairy products, including milk. Nothing magical about day 366 lets them tolerate cow milk proteins; some kids have had whole milk even before a year. However, whole milk before a year of age is not recommended. They have often been eating cheese or yogurt even as young as 9 months, but the gut for sure does better with cow milk closer to a year. From age 1 to 2, the recommendation is to use whole milk to get good fat in the diet for brain and eye development. Kids only need 16-20 ounces of whole milk, but this is a case where more is not always better. With too much milk, some kids with as minimal as 24 ounces a day, will get constipated with harder stools or can get full and not want to eat their other foods. For people still breastfeeding regularly during the day, you can count this as a good source of calcium, protein, and fat. As there is less breastfeeding, then you can increase whole milk. If constipation occurs even at 16-20 ounces a day, try to manipulate stools with foods. Some kids need a prune or a few prunes daily to compensate for the dairy effects on stools. Also, remember water to help keep stools soft.

If you find your child does not tolerate much cow milk, if any, then look to some cheese and yogurt to get the calcium, protein, and fat they need. Look for calcium in leafy greens (which go lovely in smoothies as there are not too many toddlers who love their kale!). Almond butter also has a lot of calcium, but almonds are still a choking hazard. Protein is in meats, eggs, beans, and fish. You will need to think about what daily fat you will get your kid if they are not a fan of milk. No convenient packaging for you! Avocados, butter and peanut butter on toast, coconut milk in those smoothies with almond butter and leafy greens, and coconut milk in oatmeal are some fat sources.

Eating is still the main thing kids do, although sometimes you wonder how they even survive on a few bites of white and tan foods (carb-heavy diet). Not all kids change their diets, but the 15-month mark is a typical time for toddlers to try to assert some independence, and there is no better way to do that than through food. Food and toilet are the two things we can control, and toddlers are up to the challenge! Many kids will continue to eat everything every day as they enter their toddlerdom. Other kids will change it up and eat everything one day, and other days, they will only eat four crackers. It is helpful to look at toddler eating (and all people's eating) week to week. Day to day will drive you crazy, and meal to meal will make you lose your mind! If their appetite is up and down over the week, you are doing okay.

I have learned many good phrases from mentors over the years. I used the most in my practice: "parents decide what to feed their kids, and kids decide how much to eat, do not do each other's jobs." The parents do not get to say the kids must have four more bites. The kids do not get to tell the parents they will only eat mac and cheese for dinner. If they turn their nose up at the first food offering, bear the temptation to feed your child what you know they will eat. If broccoli magically turned into grilled cheese, I may also hold out. If you make a child what you know they will eat, the child is essentially saying what the food will be, not their food job in the kid/parent food dynamic.

People, including toddlers, eat when they are hungry. Just because we say it is dinner time does not mean people will be hungry at that time. Let us all eat when we are hungry; what a different relationship we would all have with food. With respect to eating, we tend to remember the nothing days, but we forget the bottomless pit days. If you cannot remember big appetite days, then circle on the calendar any day you say in amazement, "you want more?" or "I can't believe how much you ate." When you have the four bites days, you can glance at the calendar, see all the big eating days, and feel reassured. It is important to remember that kids do not grow in a nice straight line like the growth charts you see in the pediatrician's office seem to imply. Over time kids end up following a line nicely; those lines mean something is what I found myself often telling families. However, in achieving this over time, nice even line, we tend to grow in spurts, be a bit stagnant, and have another spurt. You often look at your kids and feel they have a bit of a belly sticking out.

Then suddenly, one morning, they are wearing high water pants, the belly is flatter, and you can see their ribs. We grow out, and then we grow up.

Once the dynamics of food are established between parents and kids, parents decide what to feed the kids, and kids decide how much to eat. What to offer kids is of the utmost importance. The toddler years are when you have the most control of what kids are eating, so take it! It is easier not to get a big taste for sweet drinks/juice and sugary foods if you do not introduce them in the first place. This strategy is much easier than taking them away at age 13. Work on offering healthy foods from the beginning. I have seen some kids in the scope of a 15 min office visit plow through 2 bags of goldfish, 2 juice boxes, and a bag of fruit snacks. Controlling behavior and emotions through junk food is not a strategy for success in health or well-being. I also think variety is essential when trying to expand a toddler's palate. Try veggies raw and cooked, various dipping sauces, and the famous hiding in smoothies/soups/sauces!

With more solids and now whole milk, there is often more change in stools. Constipation, either from being sensitive to or having too much milk, is prevalent at this age. Not drinking enough water and not being a huge fan of fruits and veggies, or at least not a fan of veggies, are also potential causes of constipation. Along with the recommendations of foods to help keep the stools soft, it is important to pay attention to water and fiber intake. When you eat a piece of fruit, there is fiber in the fruit to take care of its inherent sugar. We need fiber for all the other sugars in our lives (carbohydrates like bread and pasta and pretzels and rice). You can get fiber in fiber gummies (I'm not a huge gummy fan, but the best fiber is the one that gets in!) You can also use prunes or dates daily. Another option is to use Benefiber at 3 grams a day of extra fiber for a toddler. Of course, fewer carbs and sugar are the best option. This struggle is another example of ideal and reality competing for dominance.

It is essential to be on top of what the stools are doing at this age. Kids are smart, and if it is painful to go poop, they will not go poop. Withholding stool leads to lots of problems over time. It can lead to ongoing pain, discomfort, and social implications of being the stinky kid in school from loose stool leaking around withheld stool. It takes months to over a year to fix these issues. The best treatment is prevention; avoid the desire to withhold stool.

There is not much to add for sleep as a basic rule at this age. The best way to ensure they will go back to sleep after their natural waking and stirring at night is to know how to put themselves to sleep initially at bedtime. If this has not been established yet, wait for the next time you can tolerate a few sleepless nights in a row to try to develop self-soothing at bedtime. For example, do not do this when you have finals for nursing school! Remember the second night is generally the hardest.

As the title of this chapter states, mobility is the name of the game from 12 to 18 months. Where did you go, and why are you so fast? The mantra of the early toddler years. Remember, though, mobility comes in many forms: crawling, helicopter scoot, army crawl, cruising along the furniture, walking. The idea that kids should walk before they are a year is not true. Taking independent steps is usually between 12-14 months. I find letting go and taking steps is very personality dependent. The cautious kids who want to do things right the first time may walk a little later, and kids who are carefree and adventurous may walk a little earlier. I had one kid who pulled himself to stand at 7 months of age but did not let go to take independent steps until 13 months. He was very cautious!

As mobility has increased dramatically over this time, discipline still relies on the principles of removing and distracting. They are still after eye contact and want to know which actions create the most eye contact. Another level of exploration at this age is finding a boundary and seeing what happens when they specifically go against a limit. This age of kids is spectacular at boundary-pushing, and they are in it for the long haul. What I mean by this is you, as the parent, must be more stubborn than the toddler. This resolve is no easy task since the toddler is generally more stubborn than all the adults in the house combined. The boundary-pushing is always worse the second day after you start trying to establish a boundary. Stick to your guns, you must win, and you will. You can do this!

Tidbits. It is about to pay off if you have been doing sign language for your infant/toddler. This age often has parents lamenting the fact their kid is not doing any of the signs they are so diligently teaching them. Typical examples are signs like requests for more or water or milk (always with the please motion over the chest to teach good manners!). All I can say is stick with it, and your hard work will pay off very soon. It does not take too many signs to help with communication; the key is consistently doing them as you say the words.

CHAPTER FIVE

You Never Said That Before
18 months to 2 years

By this time, you have mastered the chase. Maybe not the catching yet, but indeed the chase. Kids have been saying new words here and there until 18 months of age and understanding more of what they are hearing than expressing themselves with those words. The mobility continues to improve, and quiet in your house should be cause for alarm and a search party released to find the kids to discover what they are doing!!! At 18 months, language and voice are constant, unless they are into mischief—new words all the time but usually one word at a time. Closer to age 2, there should be a couple of words together and about half understandable to strangers. You will still get many people asking what your toddler is saying as they begin their language journey, which is normal. Just like there is a general societal idea that kids should walk before they should, I think there is a consensus that kids should talk more and earlier than they do. If there is a lack of words and understanding, you should discuss this with your medical provider. As language develops, I think the most important thing to help them along is to narrate the day as you spend time with your toddler. Talk to them about what you are looking at in the refrigerator as you make lunch and talk about putting socks on the left foot and then the right foot. Talk about it all.

It is helpful for a second (or third or fourth) time parent to remember how all kids develop at their own pace. We all tend to follow the same pattern, but the timing of this development is quite individual. When looking through developmental timelines, remember there is a mean time most of the kids will do the milestone. Still, it is a bell curve, and the normal under the curve represents a significant difference in when development occurs. It is common to find a second kid not speaking as early as the first. I discovered that we, as parents, speak less and less with the arrival of each subsequent child. You spend your whole day talking to your first kid, especially if you got to nap when they did. When you have more than one child, you are too busy ensuring everyone has eaten, has clean underwear, and has no obvious dirt on their face. There is no time for talking! You must be aware of this and try to narrate your day for subsequent children, just as you did for the first. Development is undoubtedly helped or hindered by parental interaction but remembering that kids develop on their own timelines is essential when you find inherent differences in your children's skills, competencies, and strengths. Suppose your first kid is an early talker. When you have a kid with a mean or later end of the normal time frame for language development, you will think your second kid is a moron. The same sets of genes can come together to make completely different people. These differences are present for development as well as personalities and temperament.

Eating and pooping are not changing much at this age. I strongly encourage parents to stay aware of what the stools are doing, as this is a time when some kids get very interested in potty training. As stated before, it is crucial to ensure soft stools are happening, as kids will start holding in their stools if it is painful to get them out. Diet changes are generally still the best thing to do for stool issues at this age (more water, more fiber in the diet, more veggies, fewer carbs, and less milk/cheese).

Food and toilet are the things kids can control. Along with letting the kids decide how much to eat (after we have decided what to offer), it is also important to let kids take the lead with toilet training. Potty training is a complete misnomer. We do not train them; they decide they are ready. If a parent tells you they potty trained their kid in 3 days with M&Ms, then just smile and nod. The kid was ready. It had nothing to do with the parents. If we are pushing and they do not want to do it, they will dig their heels in and say no way because they can! If your kid is interested in sitting on a potty, then go for it. However, if they fight it and want nothing to do with it, back off and let them tell you when they are interested.

Sleep can introduce another challenge: escaping out of the crib. The general answer to when you should move your toddler to a toddler bed is when they start climbing out of their crib. Better yet, move them when they are in their planning stage before execution. Of course, there is also the situation of the next baby on the way. Ready or not, a toddler bed is in your future. Some toddlers never seem to need to escape, and others will head over the crib railing the first chance they get! Again, different kids have different temperaments. Once they have decided baby jail is not for them, a toddler bed is necessary, which means middle-of-the-night visitors for the parents. My best advice is to keep putting them back in their bed when they come into your room. The first few nights will be the worst, but as with all behavioral interventions, consistency over time will have the quickest and most effective impact. This act of redirecting is an example of ideal and reality not matching; when it comes to sleep, survival is the key. I have had families tell me they put a crib mattress at the foot of the parent bed so the toddler can come in the room when needed but not interfere with everyone's sleep. We often wake up with kids in the bed without knowing how they even got there. More often, we get a swift roundhouse kick to the back, alerting us of our offspring's presence and the only thing saving them is we are only half awake. Survive; you can do it!

By this time, you have a pretty good handle on eat, sleep and poop. The anticipatory guidance and reassuring one-liners are fewer as the well visits go on. This decrease in reassurance matches the reduction in uneasiness most new parents feel over the first couple of years of life. I always encourage lists for your questions. We think we will remember, but we never remember (this also holds for teenagers and their school assignments/due dates). The list at the newborn visit is short (no sleep), and the list at the 2-week visit is long (some sleep but still clueless). By the 9-month mark, the list of questions is a little less, and by 18 months, many people feel they have a handle on this whole kid thing.

Of course, you must be careful of feeling overly confident. Kids, like life, seem to have a way of sensing our confidence and know exactly how to knock us down a few notches. A child psychologist puts forward an interesting idea with the basic concept that our kids are here to help us, the parents, work through our baggage. If you are getting many knocked down feelings, I encourage you to look at your reactions to your kid's emotions or actions and figure out what triggers you. These defeated feelings can have more to do with your own experiences and ways of thinking than what your kid did at the moment. Why are you reacting the way you do to an action which is essentially the way it is, and what happened? How we respond sets the tone and models for our children how we handle stress or difficulties. Parenting happens in the moments we are giving advice, discipline, instruction, and lecture number fill in the blank. Parenting also occurs when we are running late for school with our reaction to a moose in the driveway. Outside of Alaska, think flat tire or something that impedes your forward progress. It happens in how we communicate through a disagreement with our parenting partner and how we treat the server at a restaurant. We think we are always watching our kids, and I am here to tell you they are sneaky little buggers. They are pulling the wool over their parents' eyes all the time! They are watching us and seeing it all, no matter how sneaky we think we are.

One of my most memorable moments of an 18 month old at his well visit was when this little one crawled around on the ground in a diaper and a t-shirt. He went under the chair and tried to go to sitting from crawling. When he hit his head on the chair seat, he clear as day, in the correct context and inflection, said, "G&* D&%$@#T". They are sponges, be very careful!

Developmentally I think toddlers become little people at the age of 18 months. They can have conversations (and at some point, in the future, you will understand what those frequently strung together sounds were trying to say). They can follow some simple instructions, sometimes. I remember the first time my daughter closed the drawer after asking her to do it. I sat there in awe! They start to have opinions. These opinions are where the decision to potty train or not comes into play and the decision to eat everything one day and 4 bites the next. Opinions.

Luckily there are not too many things toddlers have much control over. Food and toilet for sure, as discussed above, and that is about all. Parenting at this age depends on not giving over control. It is much easier said than done, true for most of life, it seems, but you must win when the toddlers start to push the boundaries. And you can win!!! Pushing boundaries is their job, and most qualify as the employee of the month every month. Mean what you say and be consistent—simple words to aspire to but not always easy to obtain. When the toddler pushes the boundary and pushes and pushes and pushes, and the limit magically goes away, they will do it again in the future. If they push and push and push the boundary and it stays in place, they eventually stop pushing because it is not working. The boundary has weathered the toddler storm. The time it takes to give in to the notion they cannot change what is happening around them is variable. There are likely many reasons for this, and temperament is one of them. When you are making behavioral changes, there are some commonalities. It is often 4-5 days of the toddler pushing the boundary or changes before giving in and realizing this is how things are done now.

One of the most common outcomes of a change of boundary is a temper tantrum. The terrible 2s is a phrase that often refers to these tantrums, but I will say the tantrums usually start long before age 2. Distraction is an excellent counteraction to tantrums but if it is not helpful quickly as an end to a tantrum, ignoring and walking away is the next best thing. As soon as the tantrum stops, come back right away. Coming back at the end of a tantrum becomes hard as you do the dishes (with your side-eye firmly planted on the abandoned screaming toddler). It can take a bit to realize the tantrum has stopped. They scream, you walk away, then they quiet down, and you come back. I remember a few trips walking out of a restaurant carrying a screaming toddler, facing away from me, out to the car to have them sit in their car seat. I sat forward-facing in the front seat, waiting for the storm to pass. We went back into the restaurant after the screaming stopped, and there was no giving into whatever demand they were trying to negotiate. I have teenagers now, and the negotiations are much wordier but expressed with just as much passion. And there is no one being carried out of the restaurant. Of course, there probably would be if said teenagers would ever be seen in a restaurant with me.

My big concern here is people will think I do not see how important love and affection are in parenting and helping kids through difficult times in their lives. These tenets are the cornerstones of being a parent or a parental figure in a child's life. However, dealing with tantrums at this age with too much interaction may be counterproductive. I found from kids aged 18 months until about two and a half or so there was a need to try to see what would happen if.........? This curiosity takes form in a few basic ways. If I do this, can I get what I want (a toy, a treat, a hug, a smile, a screen)? Can I get this person in charge to look at me if I do this? Notice there is no mention of how you look at them, with or without a smile. There is no mention of the tone of vocal interaction, either happy or upset. Toddlers do not care what you say or how you say it. They only want you to be looking at them. And the most basic of all human needs, pay attention to me now!! This need for attention is something we all take with us through life. I have heard comedians and actors state they are in their profession due to their need to have people looking at them.

My daughter, at age 3, came into the middle of a group of adults at her brother's birthday party. With her hands planted firmly on her hips as her mini shoulder-width stance stood firm, she said, "nobody is talking about me!". A quick interaction in these instances about the behavior and why it is not okay or why things are happening the way they are then onto ignoring any further request at interaction. Ignoring without eye contact is the key. Especially if you are giggling at their little indignant selves. There seems to be an evolution of the tantrum somewhere near the 2 and a half to 3-year-old age that we will discuss later. The game changes for sure!

Looking at development at this age helps support the idea that they become little people. We are social animals and social development is what is on fire at this age. There is an interaction that goes beyond getting needs met with wanting to share their world with us.

Chapter Six

What Is Even Wrong?

2 years to 4 years

Up until age 2, you have been amazed by all the new things your child has done. Every day it seems you stand in awe of a new skill, word, or manipulation technique. The creativity is endless! There is now a focus on co-ordination and improvement in all these developmental areas. Speech becomes clearer, and movements become less clumsy, behavior becomes a bit less erratic. Less erratic, but behavior becomes more of a focus of your life with children; definitely. I have always told parents of premature infants to look at other babies whose birthday is near their infant's due date. The brain follows its own developmental path based on the gestational age, which is another way of saying dependent on the due date. If a baby is born two months premature, I look for them to smile at four months of age from their birth date but two months of age from their due date. In the first 2 years of life, the development outpaces anything you have ever witnessed, and something new seems to be happening every month!

Now, at age 2, they are full-fledged toddlers, continuing a slow brew of developmental gains while refining their skills. They have a little more stamina when you are at the zoo, but they still need you, at a moments notice, to carry them. It is a time in which their cuteness saves their life daily. Enjoy times they make you smile as they will make you cry. It is an up and down kind of thing with hills and valleys. Sometimes separated by weeks and sometimes separated by moments.

Age 2 is commonly referred to as the terrible two's. This period is a time of boundary-pushing. It often has started before this magical 2-year mark, but it indeed becomes a sport at this age for some kids. Much is to be said about general discipline and setting the stage for success during this time. However, there is also the child at hand and who they are personality-wise, and their development status. Dealing with behaviors needs to take all these things into account. Like sleep, there are so many behavior books out there and one will speak to you if you are in the market. A fresh perspective often helps enlighten something about your situation which may have been hidden from you up to that point. I try to focus on a few things when thinking about behaviors over the 2-3 years range.

You can break down early-stage tantrums into three categories at a basic level. One category is *I want to tell you something, and I can't.* A second is *I want that, and you will not give it to me.* The third is asking you to *pay attention to me now.* These three ideas are great places to start when tantrums are out of control. When dealing with a tantrum, consider them fitting into one of these categories.

The most significant developmental gains from the age of 2 to 3 are in the area of language. These gains are more words, more understandable, more words together, and bigger sentences. This increase in language is one of the biggest helps for the tantrum trigger of wanting to tell someone something they cannot. As speech improves, so does communication. Words are a fantastic alternative to screaming and kicking! Regarding personality, some kids are very quiet and are taking it all in; they often are not the kids acting out. The kids trying to communicate yet not understood are making the most noise about their frustrations. When needed, early interventions with services like speech therapy can make all the difference for future development and current survival for all involved. Your medical provider can help determine if this is needed. The best thing we can all do is narrate our day to support speech development. Try to redirect our kids when they are trying to say something and are getting frustrated. A simple question to help reset their lightning-speed thoughts. Sign language has helped a lot of families. Patience and time are the most definitively helpful guidance for speech issues that contribute to tantrums.

The other two tantrum triggers seem to stem from boundary-pushing. The example of I want that, and you will not give it to me is a trigger for tantrums throughout life by adults and toddlers alike. Regarding food, you will see it in hunger strikes/fights and yelling to make the broccoli turn into mac and cheese. At bedtime, you will see it in blowouts about wanting to watch one more show or read one more book. You will see opportunities everywhere and at any time when faced with sugar treats and screen time. Will I get what I want if I kick and scream loud enough? What if I go louder? What if I bang my head? What if I kick the floor? What happens if I do this in church? In the store? At home? These tantrums are where the idea of meaning what you say and being consistent comes into play.

It is helpful to have thought about these concepts early on in kids' exploration of the world around them, but now it is imperative to master these skills. If you are an empty threat, your threats will have no teeth. Mean the discipline options if the current behavior keeps up! You want to avoid them asking, "Why should I do what mom says? She never follows through on the consequence!" When your kid sees you this way, it can be a difficult identity to shake for a parent, and the kids' human nature is to do it if they can get away with it. I think it is important to remember that developmentally kids at this age are not thinking too far into the future. Complicated consequences get lost on them. If you say you will leave the store if they do not stop screaming, you better be prepared to leave the grocery store, cart in the aisle and all. (I always wondered why there were full abandoned carts at the grocery store.). And make sure you do not make this threat on a day you need toilet paper. You must follow through!

The last tantrum trigger falls at the heart of human connection; pay attention to me now! This trigger is not a reflection of how much attention a child gets. There is something in the moment they feel they need from you and are not getting. These attempts to get you to do things have been brewing for a while in very innocent explorative ways. From the 9-month-old on your hip biting your shoulder while you are talking to someone else to the 15-month-old returning to the cords and looking back at you to ensure you are watching their prohibited behavior. Now, at age 2, it is potentially a weapon to be wielded by the most indiscriminate fighters. There is an element of hurt when a child is scolded or reprimanded. There is also an element of being happy to be seen. Kids do not care about the what and how of words we use in response to the tantrum.

Boundary pushing tantrums require consistency of boundary location and implementation of consequences for going beyond the boundary. By the end of the 2nd year, you have a good handle on your little master boundary explorer and all their tricks. You have firmly established the boundaries, and sometimes, you live up to your expectations! Now they are 3. Tantrums certainly do not stop, but they do change. You will still get the typical toddler tantrum of pushing a boundary and you can respond to it by holding firm in your parental position. Distraction is a great first go-to, always. Another option is to walk away until the tantrum stops; come back immediately after it stops and discuss what is going on. However, now you get tantrums that make you scratch your head and think, "what is even wrong?"

A three-year-old is often referred to as a threenager. This idea is accurate as both ages, three and teenager, are trying to find an identity. At age three, there is a birth of an individual. Kids start saying things like "I do it" and asserting independence. Part of this independence comes from figuring out what they like and do not like. Age 3 is when my daughter very clearly told me she did not like the hand-me-down camo pants from her brother and wanted a pink pair of pants instead. This assertion of wants blossoms at this age. However, a 3-year-old is not always sure what to do with such strong desires. In one instant, they want the blue bowl; 10 minutes later, only the red one will do! When faced with a tantrum that brings up feelings of confusion in you as the parent, it is probably a tantrum that needs a little more connection to alleviate. If connection makes the tantrums worse, back away. The difference is you back away with open arms, ensuring your toddler knows this is hard and you are there when they need you. We all need a little help with our overwhelming emotions and feelings, especially at this age, as we seem to have a real conscious awareness of them. Helping can be sitting with them in their emotions, talking about their feelings, and helping them find coping mechanisms. Activity and being in the body are the best ways at this age to get out of their feelings (I like this, I do not like this, I do not know) and sensory inputs (too many choices).

My last advice for the parent of a three-year-old holds true for human beings in general. When things are off, and nothing seems to be helping mood or behaviors, always ask, "When did they last eat?". Nobody is hangrier than a three-year-old!

Chapter Seven

The Sweet Spot
4 years to Puberty

You made it through the toddler years, and now you can sit back and enjoy a bit. There is something magical about a 4-year-old. There is a sweet innocence which is the background of exploration and wonder. The years up to age 4 were filled with improved communication. After age 4, this communication is used for inquiry, questions, and wonders. Why this? How come that? These words fill your day.

Along with this increased communication comes a change in behaviors. There is some understanding, or at least some listening of explanations of boundaries we set. There is a conversation, a natural back and forth. We can learn a lot from our kids because they have not had all the social programming yet; sometimes, true wisdom comes out of little bodies. Please pay attention, though; they slip it in between the nonsense! I think having conversations with your kids is essential, not just placing kids in front of a screen. Speak to them like people, not in a baby voice.

As you enter the early childhood phase of parenting, behaviors are still the focus of life. Boundaries continue to be necessary, but there can be some involvement with the children about more of these boundaries. Choices can be beneficial when faced with a situation where a couple of different options for the child are within the limits of acceptable. The key is to ask if they want A or B. Too many choices overwhelm. You must also be sure you, as the parent, are okay with either option they choose. To avoid the answer C when given choices between A and B, you tell them the choice is A or B, and if they cannot decide, you will decide for them. My kids figured out quickly that when the choice was one granola bar or none, I would choose none every time. They are quick studies. Kids often pick things up faster than we do (except the clothes on their floor!). The consistency of boundaries is so important when it comes to behavior at any age. When we are not consistent, kids will continue trying to get us to move the boundary. If screaming and kicking get you ice cream, most of us would be on the ground right now in epic tantrum form.

Choices are clearly a good way to limit behaviors you do not like; however, we tend to give choices when we do not mean to. When my kids were much younger, I would tell them it was time to get their diaper changed followed by a quick "okay?" with clear question intonation. Adding an "okay?" to the end of the request is a perfect time for the kids to say no! We also say things like "Will you get your jacket? It is time to go." Again, a yes or no question when no is not really an acceptable answer. "Get your jacket, it is time to go" is a direction versus a question. Kids pick up on all the loopholes we provide to continue their current tasks (ahem, playing).

You have now had a few years of practice at this boundary thing, but do not be surprised when you often falter. The best we can do is strive for consistency and keep talking to our kids. Parents are human. Go easy on yourself. Grace for your kids as they are learning, and grace for yourself. You are learning too. As you enter the school years, kids come into their own personalities and temperament. You have seen glimpses of these things all along, but now the world shares in it as well. Even though many kids have been at daycare, once the school years hit, another level of social development occurs. Kids are for sure full-fledged people at this point, opinions and all. Suppose you have established a sense of security in exploring thoughts and feelings. In that case, kids will be able to receive help as they explore the ideas of fitting in and competing with others for grades or sports team spots.

Along with all the problems accompanying being a person, there is great joy in connection with your child. There is also great joy in staying in bed a bit longer on the weekend while a school-age kid gets their basic breakfast foods ready. You can ask them to get their belongings together to get ready to leave and not have to be the one following them throughout the house to ensure it happens. Of course, nothing is 100%, but you are closer to this goal most days than not at this point. This time is the sweet spot, kids become a little self-sufficient, but they still want to be around you!

School is a big part of this phase of your child's life and, therefore, your life. I had no idea figuring out kindergarten amongst all the options would be so tricky. I know it is hard to advise since schools and education constantly evolve. I write this at the 2-year mark of the coronavirus pandemic, and what school will look like on the other side of this is anyone's guess. Online school and homeschool are having a heyday, and I can see this continuing as we find our way out of a pandemic. Some basic tenets may still hold. One is to be involved. I was surprised when a parent of a 7-year-old realized for the first time they needed to go through the backpack when their child got home from school. This action is an opportunity to help kids learn organization and follow-through.

Two is to trust your knowledge of your child. Types of school settings vary as much as students themselves. There are school settings that work for some but are debilitating to others. The number of charter schools and their specialties is overwhelming sometimes. What is suitable for your neighbor's child may not be good for yours. Some schools are more structured in their settings and will do well for kids who need the structure to stay focused. However, some kids are self-sufficient and motivated and like the idea of driving their own education. There are schools out there for those kids as well. And, of course, the "old school" idea (pun intended) of a neighborhood school is an excellent option for most kids. Again, it goes back to being involved and knowing your child. You know how they will best be helped with homework, staying on top of their school, and activities, and household responsibilities.

The biggest question about school often presented itself for a group of kids who lie in-between gifted and average performance. An all-day gifted program versus one in which they are pulled from their regular classroom a few hours a week can be very intense. This more intense all day gifted program may not be a great fit even for the most academically gifted students. An excellent alternative is a language immersion school. I found this very helpful for the kids who taught themselves to read and have a good handle on the abstract idea of an alphabet and numbers before kindergarten even begins. The challenge of a new language can make up for the fact they know the work the rest of the class is doing in English (or their native language) and ideally prevent boredom. Behavior issues in school can be from not understanding the work, but they can also be born out of boredom.

Outside of the new school context, there is also a significant element of feelings starting to develop in the school-aged child as they approach puberty. Within this arena of feelings, there is a deeper intake of the outside world. There is a little less of just accepting what people say to them and more questioning what we as parents are saying. Especially if what we are telling them does not feel good to them. Sometimes parents do not tell the truth; we say we will be going to the store, then we do not. As a quick side note, a mom once told me she does not make promises; she makes plans. Plans can change. Of course, if the kid buys this or not is no guarantee on any given day, but it is a great baseline vocabulary to keep in mind. One of the main reasons a child questions what a parent is telling them is the child has their own experience. The parent had different experiences that developed their feelings in life.

Age 9-10 is where you will start to see an awakening to the outside world which is their own and may be very different from yours. There is a realization of ideas of sympathy and antipathy (likes and dislikes), good and evil, and life and death. Parents wonder what their kids may have experienced to develop these feelings. However, they are inherent in all of us as we discover the outside world has an impact on us. Until now, we have put our inner world on display to the outside—some more vocal than others. Now we start to realize the outside world can affect us. Questions like "what happens to me if you die, mommy?" seem to come out of nowhere and can shake us to our core if we are not expecting it. These thoughts are natural and a good sign of the development of children. It is preparation to be a part of the outside world without our umbrella of protection around them.

It can be very difficult to hear these things and know how to respond to the natural pulling away from the family that accompanies this realization of the world outside the family. A striving for independence shows up at this age, but the problems arise when the child takes a bigger leap than is appropriate. They may ask for things like riding their bike across town to see a friend or going independently out of the neighborhood to a park. A parent may very appropriately say the child cannot do these independent activities, and the child will respond with, "you don't let me do anything." Suppose a parent and child can sit down and decide on mutually agreed-upon independent activities. In that case, this pulling away from each other becomes more of a walk together, side by side. Around age 10 is an excellent time for a parent to leave a child at the house for 10 min while you run to the corner store to grab a gallon of milk. Clear boundaries of things like do not use the stove, do not answer the phone, and do not answer the door are requirements, and the length of time away starts small. It is also essential to know the safety of your surroundings. Would it be okay for them to walk to the mailbox alone to get the mail? The key is to decide on these activities together to allow a child their natural independent drive in a safe way.

As you emerge from this penetration of reality at age 9-10 you are inching ever closer to puberty. The ages 12-14 seem to be the peak of feelings. My son came home from school on his 12th birthday and burst into tears about something that happened with friends at school.

This big ball of feelings was a new side of him I had not seen before. At this point, there is a realization of the idea of consciousness. This awareness of the outside world is evidenced by fluctuating between what we are open to and what we shut out. This swing between the two can sometimes give you whiplash, but it is important to let this tennis match play out. Caring for our feelings is critical in developing happiness in life and an individual's feeling of self-worth. If feelings are stifled, it becomes difficult to figure out where we fit in the world. Over time, kids may decide to numb their feelings with substances and behaviors detrimental to their health and happiness.

With this consciousness begins the idea of not only how the outside world affects us but also how we start approaching the awareness that we can affect this outside world. The stage has been set for the development of a self-consciousness that takes form in the adolescent years.

Chapter Eight

Good Luck
Adolescence

You are on the home stretch now! As you wade through all the feelings of puberty, there is a light at the end of the tunnel, and hopefully, you are still strong enough to continue to move towards it. As we get into the solid teenage years, there is an emergence of ideas. There is a yearning to relate to the outside world. There is also a shift from how the world affects us to how we can affect the outside world. There is a real sense of an inner self that ideally has a strong foundation after exploring the feelings preceding this time. This sense of individuality makes it difficult to give a lot of hard and fast information regarding kids in this developmental time of life. Nothing works for most kids, let alone all kids. Luckily, as their parent, you have been with them and know them better than they would ever like to admit. Use this intimate knowledge of your children as you carve out your parenting path with them.

This inner self comes out in various ways but is there in times of conflict. The safest place to experience this conflict is in the immediate surroundings, namely with teachers and parents. This conflict helps determine the boundary of how the inner self projects into the world. As parents, we must keep this in mind. Although the angst often feels explicitly directed at us, it is really directed into the world. We are the first stop in how this will be received. It is crucial as parents to remember we play this almost brainstorming role in their lives and to make sure the kids feel supported, not abandoned. With this safe space to explore their place in the world, they can develop correct ways to interact with those around them.

The goal of this age is social connection. Our job is to help kids be part of the social context and greater mass culture with a sense of self and individuality. Ideally, this is also without a feeling of inadequacy. We must, as parents, be interested without being overbearing or judgmental (like most things in life, much easier said than done). Up to this point, we have been spoon-feeding our kids our thoughts and ideas of the world. These ideas have come from our own experiences. It is time to let our kids begin developing their thoughts and opinions based on their experiences.

Luckily at this age emerges the process of analyzing and synthesizing, which gives us an ability to overcome the feelings that stir in us. We all know, even as adults, feelings can still get the better of us. It is important kids be allowed the swings of antipathy and sympathy, dislikes and likes, and have a sense of how to work through emotions. Working through emotions ensures they do not become overwhelmed by them. We want them to be able to acknowledge feelings without dwelling. Meditation can help this process, as can journaling. They both involve letting go. Once feelings can help guide us gently versus pulling us kicking and screaming, we can use our thoughts to see things for what they are. These feelings will pass and thoughts allow us to see ourselves for who we are.

Along with discovering how we affect the outside world at this age, there is still a lot of outside world coming down on us. This oppression of life never goes away completely, but we can help foster an ability to let the world be what it is without bringing us down. One example is school and the fact the work gets more challenging, and teachers are less likely to hold your hands through the work. Junior high or middle school is the first clue you are responsible for yourself. There is not one teacher doing all the lessons and ensuring the math test, research paper, and spelling test don't fall on the same day. Once you are in junior high school and beyond, you have individual teachers for individual classes, and the teachers are not working together to ensure you are not overwhelmed. It is up to the student to know what is due when and how to best manage their time. These school years are an excellent time for parents to help them see how to manage things. I think stepping back and taking a bird's eye approach is very important. Suppose there are three tests on the same day in 3 weeks' time. In that case, it is better to do a little studying for each subject over three weeks rather than doing nothing for 2 weeks and 6 days and panicking when everything is due the next day! There are often more extracurricular activities at this age, which also play into time management. Sports may be more competitive with more time away at games or tournaments. The time away from getting schoolwork done begins to impact our lives considerably. It all needs to go on a calendar to add to the bird's eye view of life. You may discover the schedule is too full when you see it all written out. It is easy to compartmentalize life and not even notice how all the activities relate together until you put things down on paper and see it in black and white.

There is a fine line between helping teenagers and interfering with their lives. It is best, to be honest and straightforward when speaking and listen when they speak. Abstract thoughts are a new thing for kids at this age, and if we are too closed off or overbearing, there is no help for them to navigate these new thought processes. There can be no beating around the bush, be direct and honest with compassion. What seems like the end of the world to them may not matter much to you, but they matter to them, keep that in your thoughts.

Chapter Nine

The First Seven Years
A plea for minimal screens

A primary purpose of the first seven years of life is to master the physical body. When a child is ready for school, they must know where their body is in space without thinking about it. These thought forces need to be accessible for paying attention to the teacher and learning new concepts. Everything is new, including such basic ideas like placing lines together to make a letter with a sound associated with it. This mastery of the physical body comes from movement and living in the limbs. Suppose we are properly integrated with our bodies. This makes it possible to eventually touch the middle top of our head without looking in the mirror. We know where we are in space. If we are not fully integrated in our bodies, we may feel slightly off-balance while sitting in a chair and have a need to squirm and move to feel ourselves in space and re-orient. It is hard to pay attention when you are constantly worried you will be falling off the chair!

I like to think of the human in a threefold way with the head being the nerve-sense area and it is all about sense impressions. The gut and limbs are the metabolic pole, opposite of the nerve-sense pole, and this is where the doing of life lives. Movement and digestion reign supreme here. The middle realm is the heart and lungs, representing balance, in-breath and out-breath, pump and fill. This middle realm can help balance the top and bottom poles, the head and the gut/limbs. So often, these three divisions of the human are out of balance. When we are in our heads too early, we are sensing everything around us. If our lower pole is not developed, we have no way to digest all we are sensing. This inability to deal with the world around us happens when small children live on screens. They have a lot of sense impressions but are unsure what to do with them. The ability to digest things means we can take the impressions of the outside world and add something of ourselves to them to incorporate them into our lives. Young kids have not had the experiences to be able to add things yet. The first seven years are about developing this digestion ability.

We can see the importance of developing this lower pole later in life when we start having our own thoughts and new ideas. Suppose we are not allowed to have imagination in our younger years. Our ability to come up with something new suffers. Screens do not interact with kids; even the learning games have specific rules. Toys often do one thing and can hinder any imaginative thoughts from developing. My kids' favorite "toys" were a box of silk scarves. These scarves became capes and flags and armor and a rope. A stick and rock outside can be a myriad of things, not just a toy that lights up when you press a specific button.

There is general knowledge of the five senses: touch, vision, smell, hearing, and taste. I like to think of senses in a broader sense, no pun intended. There are lower senses of life sense, proprioception/balance, movement, and a deeper meaning of touch. This more profound idea of touch is the most basic of them, as it tells us where we end and the world begins. We wake up to the outside world and begin to have a conscious awareness of boundaries, of ourselves. When you touch the counter, you sense a change in yourself at the fingertip and feel pressure on your skin. When we see our kids stumble, our first instinct is to give them a big hug or rub the bump. It grounds us. When a toddler or child cannot go to sleep as they are squirming all around, I have had a lot of luck getting them to settle into their body through touch. This touch allows them to be more still. Something a mentor of mine calls toothpaste treatment at bedtime can help. Gently squeeze the arms from the armpit down to the fingers and do a gentle pulling stroke down each finger to settle them into their whole body. You can do this with the legs to the toes as well. Another grounding action is reading a book at bedtime while they are wrapped up in a blanket like a burrito. Once a child feels grounded throughout their whole body, it is easier to release to go to sleep.

The next sense up the chain is a general life sense. Do we feel good, or do we feel bad? When we are not feeling secure or safe in the world, it is challenging to concentrate, learn new information, or even pay attention. A good life sense is a balance of the autonomic nervous system. We are not in a state of fight or flight when this system is in balance. We are also not disengaged either. This sense is a warning system and alerts us when changes are needed. Feeling bad helps us realize we need to do something else to feel good. Of course, in today's society of stuff, media, and substances, many things make us feel good. Still, in reality, they take us further away from our life sense. Being in touch with our bodies, feelings, and thoughts will help us achieve the life sense balance we all strive for.

There are concrete things to help with such a nebulous idea of a good life sense. Warmth is essential for this. When you are warm, you can be fully present. The attention is on the temperature when you are too cold or too hot. Warmth is a contentedness allowing consciousness or awareness to be directed to other places. Nutrition is, of course, also crucial to a good life sense. Not only does the presence of food and drink matter, but the quality of nutrition is also important. We are meant to digest real food. The processed foods ingested are extra work for us to digest. A basic tenet of life has always been food is thy first medicine. Although what is convenient and affordable is often the worst food for us, I implore you to do your best. An actual vegetable whenever you can!

Breathing is another way to develop a good life sense. When we are tense and nervous, we hold our breath. With a good deep breath and prolonged exhale, the shoulders immediately relax. Taking deep breaths can often lead to hyperventilating, so I like to give specific instructions such as breathing in for 4 seconds, holding for 4 seconds, and breathing out slowly for 4 full seconds. Older kids can do a little longer. It is also important to count the time on your fingers, or we will usually speed it up. Movement is also a way to get us into our bodies and out of our minds. Noncompetitive and rhythmical movements are settling to the soul. Think patty cake or skipping rope or hopscotch. Children seem to innately know this as they will often get very restless when there has not been enough physical activity.

Sleep is so important, and no one seems to get enough. When our schedule is too full, our ability to deal with sensations we are exposed to and get a good night's sleep is affected. Screens in the room also affect our ability to sleep, probably through electromagnetic effects and the temptation to live in our heads while watching. Remember, we can let go easier once we fully integrate into the body during the day. Routines and rhythm allow us to know what is coming without nervousness about what is next. And finally, what gives us the most stable life sense is feeling unconditional love. There is a freedom to live when we know we will always have a safety net of love to fall back on when we need it.

Moving on from a general life sense is movement. When we feel good in our movements, we have a sense of inner life. Movement deals with the changes in the configuration of the body. We can feel inside that we are moving, and we are the ones directing movement. I make a plan to move, and I move. A connection between the head and the limb occurs.

The last lower sense is proprioception. We can translate this into moving versus stillness in relation to the outside world. It is comforting to be able to feel the space around you. People with a fear of heights are not great at feeling this space around them when standing near the edge. They do not fill the space below them and could just tumble into it at any moment. As one who experiences heights this way, it has always been strange to me that I feel I might fall right off the cliff even though I know I would not plan on taking the step necessary to fall. A good sense of proprioception and balance allows us to share our space with others. As stated earlier, another benefit to a good sense of balance is when we know where we are in space, our thoughts are free to think of higher things. We can develop this with balance beam walking, jump rope, and skipping. A sense of equilibrium in our body will translate into a sense of equilibrium in our hearts and mind.

The first seven years are when these lower life senses integrate into our beings. Still, they are things we need to readdress when feeling off in any way throughout our lifetime. When these are out of sync, higher senses of thought, words, and relating to another as an individual become difficult. Returning to basics of the lower senses is always a good first step when feeling off at any age.

Chapter Ten

It's Always the Poop

At least almost always

I always said if I ever wrote a book, I would have a chapter called It's Always the Poop! It will likely be a short chapter, but I want to make sure to put my signature on this book. Any nurse or colleague I have ever worked with has repeatedly heard me say this phrase. I based my well visit questions, beyond what each family wanted to specifically address at the visit, on what I saw kids for during various acute illness visits. I found the issue was often a backup of stool, causing many problems for children. At least the ones that triggered a visit to the doctor. I think it is a topic families avoid discussing. Parents would often respond to the stool questions with answers like, "I am not part of that anymore now that they can wipe themselves."

It is not a popular topic to talk about, although it is so important to be paying attention.

I have seen a backup of stool affect behaviors, as well as causing more physical complaints. Behavior issues are complicated and have many layers generally. Still, I often found cleaning out stool led to better behaviors. If we are honest, even as adults, we all feel better after a good poop!

The physical complaints which lead me to consider a backup of stool at the heart of the issues range from expected to surprises. The most common complaint is, of course, abdominal pain. A parent's first thought is appendicitis whenever a kid says his belly hurts. The majority of times when there is belly pain it is not appendicitis, but we must consider what needs immediate attention. Appendicitis usually starts around the belly button and moves to the lower right side. Kids are not hungry and have pain with movement (either jumping up and down or when you tap their feet when laying down or going over bumps when riding in the car). Of course, not all kids read the books and can present in different ways. Toddlers are notorious for not following the rules! If belly pain is progressively getting worse, even if these other signs are not present, it is a good idea for someone to see them and lay hands on the belly. The exam is very telling. A surgeon once told me constipation pain shows up at the emergency room in the early AM hours as the intestines wake up for the day and push against a belly full of stool. On the flip side, appendicitis usually shows up in the emergency room late at night after the pain has worsened all day, and they cannot take it anymore. Of course, this is not always true, but an interesting idea to keep in mind.

The location of the pain and the severity are very telling when trying to figure out if you need to do anything about it either at home or taking them to the doctor. Location is important because it goes along with the organs in the abdominal cavity. Upper right-side pain is more concerning of a gall bladder issue (not too common but can happen in kids, especially teenagers). Lower right-side pain is concerning for appendicitis. Upper middle stomach pain is more concerning for reflux or gastritis (stomach irritation). Of course, these locations do not mean a bigger problem, but it makes the exam much more critical. There can be upper right and left side pain from constipation as the stool gets stuck in the corners of the large intestine as it winds its way through the abdominal cavity. Still, when there are these more specific locations of pain, it should drive you to be seen sooner rather than later, especially if the pain is progressively worsening. The pain of constipation is often much vaguer and generally not at any specific point. When you ask a kid with constipation to point with one finger where it hurts, they usually take that one finger and move it all over the belly. It can be around the belly button but does not then move down to the right side over time like the pain of appendicitis will do. Toddlers can even complain of back pain when there is constipation. Back pain is an unusual complaint in all kids. I would always say a medical provider should see them before chalking it up to constipation alone.

Constipation can also affect appetite but this is more indolent or slow to progress than the pain associated with an acute illness. When you think about it, the appetite may have decreased over time but not reduced enough to send up worry signals. I have seen kids with long-standing constipation slowly drift down the growth curve with their weight and then recover their line when they are cleaned out and ready to fill up again.

The qualities of the pain are also very telling. What often happens with constipation is the kid says, "My tummy hurts," and they run off and play. You do not think anything of it as they are running away from you quicker than you can even register worry. However, one day you think to yourself, "they have been saying that a lot lately." This may be a sign of constipation. It rarely wakes kids up in the middle of the night, although, as stated before, the early AM hours may be an issue for these kids. Just as the location of the pain is vague, so is how they describe it. It is a dull ache, but there can be doubling over sharp pains as the intestines stretch out to accommodate a larger stool load. Even if they have horrible doubling over pain, they run off to play right after it passes. You should seek medical attention immediately if they appear sedated after having doubled-over pains. The distress associated with gas can also be very sharp and short-lived, with normal life in between. The stool makes gas, so the more stool there is, the more gas there may be. A bright 9-year-old boy once told me a fart is a poop knocking on the door to come out. Such wise words!

The stool itself is also a clue to constipation being the culprit. The stools can be huge and difficult to pass. I would often ask parents if they say to themselves, "how did that come out of you?!?" A larger size stool may signify a significant stool burden in the last part of the intestine and can be a marker of more behind it. Small pellet stools can also signify there is a backup of stool and small pieces of stool are breaking off. Oddly enough, diarrhea can also be a sign of constipation. When the stool gets backed up enough, there can be softer stool behind the stool burden which starts to leak around. This leakage is most concerning when the looser stools leak uncontrollably. Not all stool stains in the underwear are from poor wiping; some are leaking-related.

The time between stools is undoubtedly something to inquire about, but there is a special note about infants. Constipation in infants is more about the consistency of the stools and less about the frequency. If the baby is eating well, seems comfortable, and the stool is soft when they go, they are less likely to be constipated. This scenario is especially true in breastfed infants, who sometimes are once-a-week poopers! For infants, small nugget stools are more concerning, as is pain or decreased appetite between stooling.

There are also symptoms related to constipation that may not be as obvious. In the abdomen region, upper belly pain can be constipation. Things start to come up when we get so backed up and the food we swallow feels like it can't go down. The result can be reflux or heartburn symptoms. The other odd complaint that may be related to constipation is urine leaking. This leaking can happen in boys and girls, but in girls, it often leads to recurrent rashes in the vaginal area. These rashes can be seen as red irritation or even can develop into skin yeast infections. If your child has a lot of vaginal rashes or urine leaking, then ask about the poop. The stool burden can push on the bladder and make it spasm and leak some urine, not because the bladder is full but because of the outside pressure. This external pressure can block the complete emptying of the bladder too, and when urine sits in the bladder for prolonged periods of time, it can get infected. Urine infections in boys are unusual and need to be evaluated by a medical provider, as do recurrent infections in females or infections of either gender when infants. However, the urologist will work on treating constipation when no underlying pathology is evident after evaluation.

When you are at the point of symptoms from constipation, seeing a medical provider is important to rule out other causes and give you more immediate relief of the stool back up. However, there are things you can do preventively to help avoid these situations in the first place. The first thing is to be aware. Every doctor's kid is familiar with being quizzed about their poop, even at uncomfortable times like the dinner table. For such a primary function of the human body, people are very reluctant to talk about it. Even 9-year-old boys who talk about poop and farts all day long get embarrassed and clam up when asked about it directly. It is okay to tell your doctor and parent what your poop looks like and know we all look in the toilet after we poop. You are not alone!

The second thing is to think about the diet you are eating. Milk is the first culprit causing constipation. I had a telemedicine visit with a kid with abdominal pain who barely would sit still to be on the camera. He was off playing and running and jumping around. I saw him in the background when I asked him to return to the camera so his dad could push on his belly. He was standing in front of an open refrigerator while guzzling from a gallon jug of milk. Aha! The answer presented itself. When you start getting up to 24 ounces of milk a day and higher, most of us will get constipated unless we balance things out with other foods. Cheese is the other player, a staple in toddler's, and children and, let's face it, most people's diets.

After dairy, I found lack of fiber is a big problem in kids' diets. This lack of fiber is probably an issue for many adults as well. The fiber in our diet from fruits and veggies helps us deal with the sugars in our life. The fiber in fruit can help with the sugars of the fruit. However, we have a lot of other sugars in our diet, and even the best veggie eater has a hard time getting enough fiber. Start looking at labels and know even what we consider healthy foods can be loaded with added sugars. Flavored yogurt is as bad as a candy bar regarding added sugars. The sugars are not all from the fruit. I am not a big fan of gummies as they also have a minimal amount of added sugars, but the best fiber is the one that gets in so gummy fibers are an option. You can mix fiber powders with water, which can help, especially in the hard-to-get-good veggies in years. For some of us, this minimal veggie phase is still in full swing as adults. The third thing to think about is water. Most moms' answers to their kids having belly complaints are to sit on the toilet and drink more water. Moms know (and dads too).

The last thing to talk about regarding constipation is the idea of withholding stool. Withholding, especially in toddlers, often shows up when kids have a painful experience with stooling and decide that if a stool is probably going to hurt, they can hold it in. The urge to go passes as the intestines accommodate a stool load so we can continue our day. This intentional act can happen at any time in life, but toilet-training time is one of the most common. Another time I see withholding is when entering kindergarten or any time people do not want to use a public restroom in general. It is important to be aware of the stooling patterns to avoid this. If kids are afraid to go poop in public, have active toilet time where they sit on a toilet for 10 min or so daily. This sitting is ideally 20 min after a meal or right when they get home from school, even if they do not think they have to go. I usually say to take a book, pretend to be dad, and hang out for a bit. Make sure there is a place to rest the feet. Clenching every muscle in your bum to avoid falling in the toilet while balancing is counterproductive to passing stool. Withholding can lead to stool leaking; once you get to this point, it is challenging to fix.

The idea of prevention techniques reminds us constipation is a slowly developing process. The further you get into it, the more complicated and time-consuming it is to reverse the course. It usually takes months to get to a point where you see a lot of symptoms, and it will take months to get total relief. It takes time for the intestines to return to a smaller size and the stretching to improve. It also takes a reasonable period of soft stools to eliminate the fear of stooling. Once this fear is gone, withholding, ideally, is gone with it. Even if you are not dealing with withholding and leaking, it will take time to heal from constipation. Soft stool for a couple of weeks may not do the trick, so when your provider has you on a stool softener for a few months, they mean it! Making basic diet changes is also essential so it does not come back.

I guess this was not short after all. My sister asked who knew there was so much to talk about with poop? Apparently, I did!

CHAPTER ELEVEN

Kids Are Weird
My favorite diagnosis

There were so many visits when I was a practicing pediatrician where the family saw me with a complaint for which I had no answers. What I realized is kids are weird! You must approach kids' complaints and actions with a sense of "how does this affect life?" As an example, we all have times of anxiety, but does it debilitate you or your child? Is it impossible to go to school or a job or maintain relationships with friends or family? If these fundamental parts of life are affected, you must address them more aggressively. If not, you can approach these things more gently to avoid them becoming more problematic.

Kids also have varying degrees of awareness of their bodies. There are times they feel every little twinge and pang. Again, how does it affect life? I often could not give a clear reason behind what they were describing, but I would know enough not to be worried. Sometimes it is enough to know what things are not as it is to understand what they are.

Kids are weird; sometimes, you must move on without a clear answer, and things will be just fine. Trust your gut and seek medical attention when you need to. If a provider has thoughtfully considered possibilities, this can often be enough to reassure you. However, get another opinion if the mommy/daddy gut is still nagging at you. Once you have done your due diligence to calm your worries, continue monitoring for any interference with life. Otherwise, remember, kids are weird.

CHAPTER TWELVE

Sincere Honesty

From one parent to another

As I write this book, my family is in chaos and turmoil. So much so that I started feeling fraudulent in advising parents. Who am I to say how anyone should do things? I sure have not been able to raise a perfect family. But the truth is no family is perfect. Just because my family and I have had struggles does not discount the information I have shared thus far. I strongly feel the information should be shared. I also do not want anyone to think we, as human beings, will always do things perfectly. There will be good days and bad days. We can only take things one day at a time, sometimes one hour at a time. My kids and I have struggled with depression and anxiety, especially during a pandemic. There have been trips to the emergency room for suicidal ideation. There was a visit from the office of children's services because an ER mental health provider disagreed with our child losing an opportunity due to poor behaviors at home. I did not think I could feel like any more of a failure as a parent.

The last few months have taught me the importance of honesty. I can finally see a path ahead by being honest with myself and my family. Bringing things to the light makes this path visible, even if it is only one step at a time. We can heal and be whole only when we bring the dark to the light.

The truth is……. How does this sentence end for you? It has led me to see I am an addict. I have a brain disease which leads me to look for the next dopamine hit. I have certainly used various substances and behaviors in the past to make myself feel better. I have never had the rock bottom moment obvious to anyone else. I did not lose my job. I have not had to file for bankruptcy. However, my family has been on the verge of falling apart, and I have spent many days feeling miserable. I see this misery in my kids' faces now, which also breaks my heart. I do not want them to live in the shame I have had for years.

My most current drug of choice is sugar. Although I am 8 days sugar-free at the time I write this (I know it is not long, but every day counts!). I speak in the present tense as I understand addiction to be a chronic and progressive disease. I am also keenly aware addiction will present itself in many forms. These forms include drugs, food, sugar, work, sex, pornography, screens, and social media. The list goes on. We live in a world of overabundance and over-stimulation and more and now. Living without the need to dull my feelings has already given me the freedom to feel. As hard as it is sometimes, feelings are a part of life; they are not always roses, sunshine, and unicorns. They are often barbed wire, monsters, and dark clouds. And this is okay. When we allow ourselves to feel all the feelings, we allow ourselves the opportunity to let them pass and move on about our day. Trying to cover them up all the time is exhausting. The lies we tell ourselves and others are exhausting.

None of us are perfect as people or parents. We just do the best we can, with honesty and good intentions. We will all make mistakes, but these mistakes are an opportunity to grow and deepen this experience in the world. My favorite phrase I try to apply to all endeavors in my life is earnest, heartfelt striving. With this as your guide, you are the best parent you can be for your kids. You are the best you that you can be as well.